12 STORIES ABOUT
HELPING AFTER
A DISASTER

by Patricia Hutchison

STORY LIBRARY
MORE TO EXPLORE

www.12StoryLibrary.com

12-Story Library is an imprint of Bookstaves.

Photographs ©: Tino Adi P/Shutterstock.com, cover, 1; United Nations/PD, 4; Sara_Escobar/ Shutterstock.com, 4; Odyssey Creative/YouTube, 5; Larry Downing/Reuters/Newscom, 6; ABC News/YouTube, 7; Michael Tippett/CC2.0, 8; Fajrul Islam/Shutterstock.com, 8; Sgt. Craig Anderson/US Army, 9; ReasonTV/YouTube, 10; RonTech3000/Shutterstock.com, 11; s_bukley/Shutterstock.com, 12; TODAY/YouTube, 12; MLB/YouTube, 13; US Dept. of Housing and Urban Development (HUD)/PD, 14; Houston Life/YouTube, 15; Jocelyn Augustino/ FEMA/PD, 16; Jocelyn Augustino/FEMA/PD, 17; Al Jazeera English/YouTube, 18; s_bukley/ Shutterstock.com, 18; TED/YouTube, 19; Yichuan Cao/Sipa/Associated Press, 20; Destinee Klyne/The Canadian Press, 21; Ilya Andriyanov/Shutterstock.com, 21; One America Appeal/ YouTube, 22; One America Appeal/YouTube, 23; Larissa Wohl/YouTube, 24; Technical Sgt. Daniel St. Pierre/US Air Force, 25; Loco Steve/CC2.0, 25; Mike Moore/FEMA/PD, 26; digitalped/YouTube, 27; mangostock/Shutterstock.com, 28; a katz/Shutterstock.com, 29

ISBN
9781632357441 (hardcover)
9781632358530 (paperback)
9781645820291 (ebook)

Library of Congress Control Number: 2019938653

Printed in the United States of America
October 2019

May 21
J

363.34

About the Cover
Volunteers in Indonesia unload supplies for victims of the 2018 tsunami.

Access free, up-to-date content on this topic plus a full digital version of this book. Scan the QR code on page 31 or use your school's login at 12StoryLibrary.com.

Table of Contents

UNICEF: Helping Children after Earthquakes in Mexico

UNICEF stands for United Nations International Children's Emergency Fund. Its name was later shortened to the United Nations Children's Fund. Its mission is to help meet the basic needs of all children.

Two earthquakes rocked Mexico in 2017. The first one struck the Pacific Coast on September 7. Twelve days later, a second quake shook central Mexico. Nearly 5 million children were affected by the quakes. UNICEF responded quickly, providing food and medicine.

In Mexico, UNICEF volunteers supplied clean drinking water. They gave hygiene kits to nearly 3,600 families. The kits held soap, towels, toothpaste, and other necessities. Volunteers also handed out blankets and raincoats. Workers shared

Workers in Mexico City remove rubble caused by the 2017 earthquake.

information with parents. They told them how to protect their children and keep their family from being separated.

The next step was to get children back into their classrooms. Over 5,000 schools were damaged or destroyed by the quakes. UNICEF worked with partners to create temporary schools. Within 72 hours after the quake, children began learning again.

UNICEF volunteers passed out kits called School-in-a Box. They contained workbooks, pencils, and scissors. Each kit had enough supplies for a teacher and 40 students. The lid of the box could be used for a chalkboard. UNICEF partners supplied books in Spanish. With these tools, teachers were able to set up classrooms almost anywhere.

THINK ABOUT IT

After a disaster, UNICEF works hard to get children back to school. Why is it so important that children's education not be interrupted?

190+

Number of countries UNICEF serves

- The organization was started in 1946.
- The United Nations voted to create it after World War II.
- Its mission was to help children in countries devastated by the war.

Peyton Robertson: Inventing Sandless Sandbags

Peyton Robertson is a native of Florida. He grew up in the path of damaging hurricanes. In 2012, he watched floods from Superstorm Sandy wreck the Northeast coast of the United States. People filled sandbags to keep the water out of their homes. But the bags were heavy and hard to carry. Gaps between them let the water flow through. Robertson thought there must be another way. So, at the age of 11, he designed a better sandbag.

Robertson's sandbag doesn't use sand. Instead, it contains a polymer. When it's dry, the bag is lightweight and easy to carry. When it's soaked in water, the polymer swells. Then bags can be stacked to form a barrier.

Peyton Robertson with President Barack Obama at the 2014 White House Science Fair.

WANTING ONLY TO HELP OTHERS

Many inventors apply for patents on their products. The legal documents prevent others from copying their designs. Robertson applied for a different kind of patent for his sandbag. It is called an open patent. He wants others to be able to use and improve his design.

$25,000
Amount of money Peyton Robertson won for his sandbag design

- Robertson won first place in the 2013 Discovery Education 3M Young Scientist Challenge.
- He was named America's 2013 Top Young Scientist.
- He calls his invention the Sandless Operational Sandbag (SOS).

At first, Robertson didn't know how to keep the bags from floating away. He added salt. The first time he tried it, the bags didn't swell as much. He experimented until he found the right amount to add. The salt makes the bags heavier than the surging sea water. They stay in place.

To eliminate the gaps between the bags, Robertson created fasteners that lock together. They hold the bags in place as they expand. When the bags dry, they flatten out. They can be stored, ready for use during the next storm.

A deflated SOS with illustrations of salt vs. polymer and the SOS inflating as water rises.

Doctors Without Borders: Caring for Tsunami Victims

In May 1968, a group of young doctors reinvented the idea of emergency relief. They decided to ignore political and religious borders. They wanted to serve victims of wars and other disasters, wherever they were needed. Eventually the group became known as Médecins Sans Frontières, or MSF. In English, they are Doctors Without Borders. The organization was officially created in December 1971. Today it has offices in 21 countries around the world.

On December 22, 2018, the Anak Krakatau volcano erupted in Indonesia. Part of the volcano slid into the ocean. This triggered a powerful tsunami that struck the coast of Indonesia. Waves up to 10 feet high (3 m) battered the islands of Java and Sumatra. Over 400 people were killed. More than 7,000 others were injured.

MSF went to work immediately. The medical team supported health

Tsunami survivors survey the damage.

centers that were damaged by the tsunami. Volunteers worked with staff to care for injured patients. The most common problems were muscle trauma and skin infections.

300

Number of MSF volunteers in 1971

- That number included the 13 founding doctors and journalists.
- Doctors, nurses, and other medical staff joined the organization.
- Their mission is simple: to provide medical aid where it's needed most.

Many survivors evacuated to higher ground. Some were injured trying to escape the rising water. But they could not reach medical centers. MSF sent out a mobile clinic to help them. The clinic reached 15 villages. Staff cleaned and dressed wounds. They treated illnesses.

But many streets were blocked. Sometimes the team was not able to reach the people in need. So medical staff coordinated treatments by phone. After roads were cleared, MSF volunteers made follow-up visits. They checked on patients to make sure they were healing.

Airbnb: Sheltering Victims of Hurricane Matthew

In early October 2016, Hurricane Matthew approached the US East Coast. Thousands of families had to evacuate their homes. Many found shelter with their smartphones. They contacted Airbnb. This is a company that rents vacation homes through its website. Airbnb activated its Disaster Response program for victims of Matthew.

The Airbnb Disaster Response program began in 2013. After Superstorm Sandy hit New York in 2012, an Airbnb host from Brooklyn wanted to help. He asked if there was a way to offer his home for free. Over 1,000 other New Yorkers welcomed victims into their homes. Now the company has a full-time disaster response team. They work with local emergency management officials. Together they decide when to activate the system. They also decide which hosts to contact and in what areas.

Airbnb also offered their Disaster Response program to people in Texas and Louisiana after Hurricane Harvey in 2017.

airbnb

Hurricane Harvey
Texas and Louisiana

If you have available housing in the area indicated on the map, please consider making your home available.

f ✓ ✉ ···

Do you need free housing?

Find shelter

Are you able to help?

Sign up your home

Hosts in the regions marked on the map are opening their homes for free from **August 23, 2017** to **September 25, 2017** for the following groups:

• Displaced neighbors

10

A GLOBAL EFFORT

Airbnb hosts have helped victims of more than 20 disasters around the world. They helped during flooding in Louisiana. Many hosts opened their homes after earthquakes shook Ecuador and Japan. They also responded after terrorist attacks in Paris and Brussels.

Before Matthew made landfall, Airbnb emailed hosts in safe zones near affected areas. It asked them if they wanted to help. The site matched people who need shelter with hosts located nearby. The guests stayed for free until officials gave the all-clear in their hometowns. The program also helped disaster relief volunteers find housing near the places where they were working.

3,000
Number of homes Airbnb offered during Hurricane Matthew

- The homes were located in Florida, Georgia, and South Carolina.
- Airbnb waived the service fees the hosts would have normally paid.
- People who had never hosted with Airbnb signed up to help.

California Strong: Raising Money for Wildfire Victims

see the damage. His house was charred, but it was still standing. His neighborhood looked like a war zone.

Several deadly wildfires spread through thousands of acres of California in the fall of 2018. Many families lost everything. Driving through the canyons, Braun was shocked by the damage. He texted two of his teammates, Christian Yelich and Mike Moustakas. The men created a text chain that included other pro athletes. Together, they made a promise. When the fires were out, they would start a charity.

The group came up with a name. They created a logo and partnered with the YMCA. Then California Strong went to work to raise money. Before long, they had collected over $300,000 in donations through their website. They held an auction. People bid on items such as a round of golf with a pro athlete. Other

At 3 a.m. on November 9, 2018, Ryan Braun had to evacuate his home. The Woolsey Fire was spreading toward the MLB player's house in California. Later, he returned to

97,000

Number of acres destroyed in the Woolsey Fire

- Three people died and 1,600 buildings were destroyed.
- The Camp Fire in Northern California started the same day as the Woolsey Fire. It was the deadliest wildfire in over 100 years.
- Eighty-eight people died in the Camp Fire and 150,000 acres were destroyed.

stars donated guitars and autographed merchandise to be auctioned.

The organization hosted a Thanksgiving-style dinner for victims of the fires. They handed out gift bags. In January 2019, they hosted a celebrity softball game to help the cause. So far, California Strong has raised over $1 million. The money is distributed as grants to help victims rebuild. The campaign is still going on. Its leaders hope that whenever tragedy strikes in their home state, California Strong will be there to help.

Ryan Braun (right) awards a check to a family who lost their home in the California wildfires.

CALIFORNIA STRONG	Date 01-13-19
	112
Pay to the Order of **The MacLeod Family**	$ 10,000⁰⁰
Ten Thousand and 00/100	Dollars

"Mattress Mack": Turning Stores into Shelters

Jim McIngvale woke up on August 27, 2017, to three feet of water. Hurricane Harvey had made landfall two days earlier near Houston, Texas. His house had flooded. As he drove to one of his furniture stores, he saw the damage all around him. He just had to help. His stores had been built to be flood-proof. They had bathrooms and restaurants. They also had plenty of mattresses. McIngvale was known as "Mattress Mack."

McIngvale posted a message on social media. He told people they could stay at his stores for free. He asked those who were trapped to contact him. Then he sent his moving trucks out into the city. They brought in over 200 people. Soon, nearly 400 took shelter in both stores. McIngvale allowed them to bring their pets. He and his volunteers provided free meals for the evacuees.

"Mattress Mack" with his employees.

200

Number of people who stayed in Jim McIngvale's stores in 2005 during Hurricane Katrina

- Hurricane Harvey wasn't the first time "Mattress Mack" turned a store into a shelter.
- In 2005, he helped people who had fled to Houston from New Orleans.
- McIngvale knew that being together in the same space would be helpful to the people from New Orleans. They wouldn't feel they had to weather the storm alone.

McIngvale is no stranger to disaster. In 2009, someone set his warehouse on fire. He lost millions of dollars of furniture. But support from his Houston customers kept him in business. Sheltering victims of Harvey was a way to give back to his community.

THINK ABOUT IT

Jim McIngvale repaid his customers for the kindness and support they gave him when he needed it. Have you ever repaid a kindness? What did you do?

Caterpillar, Inc.: Cleaning Up after a Tornado

A Caterpillar excavator cleans debris from a flattened home.

Early morning skies were sunny over Washington, Illinois, on November 17, 2013. Later, a warm front from the Gulf met with a cold front from the Great Lakes. The collision caused a disaster. At about 11 a.m., a powerful tornado tore through the city. The storm lasted only a half hour. But it left the city in a pile of rubble.

Mounds of debris blocked the roadways. First responders could not get through to help injured victims. Large machines were needed to clear the wreckage. Washington had an advantage. The headquarters of Caterpillar, Inc. was close by. The company is a leading manufacturer of construction and mining equipment. They had the machines, and their employees wanted to help.

Caterpillar employees took diesel fuel, gas, and as much water as they could get. First, they cleared the roads. Then they went door-to-door.

They used the machines to help residents sift through what was left of their homes. Some people found precious keepsakes that hadn't been destroyed. Every day, at least two Caterpillar employees worked around the clock. Without their support, it would have taken much longer to clean up the city.

CATERPILLAR DONATED TO FIRST RESPONSE TEAM AMERICA

First Response Team America has helped with dozens of US disasters. They helped residents in Washington, Illinois, after the tornado struck in 2013. In 2014, Caterpillar, Inc. donated two track loaders to First Response Team. The equipment helps communities take the first steps toward cleanup after a disaster.

190

Maximum wind speeds in miles per hour (305.7 km/hr) during the tornado

- Nearly 600 homes in Washington, Illinois, were destroyed.
- The storm left 564,000 cubic yards (431,209 cubic meters) of debris.
- A sign reading "Washington" was found 90 miles (145 km) away.

Chef José Andrés: Millions of Meals in Puerto Rico

Chef José Andrés serving after Hurricane Maria.

Chef José Andrés first organized World Central Kitchen (WCK) in 2010. The group traveled to Haiti to install clean cooking equipment there. In 2013, the organization expanded. It added a network of 140 professional chefs. The group became a kind of "Chefs Without Borders" operation. They traveled all over the world, helping to make positive changes in kitchens and cooking methods. When Hurricane Maria smashed into Puerto Rico in 2018, WCK added disaster relief to its mission.

Andrés and his WCK team arrived in Puerto Rico a few days after Maria struck. There was no electricity anywhere. The island was devastated. Crops had been destroyed. The group began serving doctors and nurses in hospitals in

A GIANT RESTAURANT

Among the 18 kitchens WCK used in Puerto Rico was an NBA arena. It took only a few hours to get it up and running. Volunteers cooked thousands of meals there. They also used it to store all the food that was bought or donated.

San Juan. The team also worked in a restaurant owned by one of Andrés's friends. They fed a few thousand people there.

Soon calls started coming in from all over the island. Everyone was hungry. Andrés knew one kitchen would not be enough. So WCK expanded their operation. They took charge of kitchens in restaurants and schools. Food trucks joined in the effort. Volunteers served over 150,000 meals a day.

Andrés and his group stayed in Puerto Rico for a year. In all, they served over 3 million meals to victims of Maria.

30,000
Number of ham sandwiches WCK volunteers made each day

- Nearly 500 people worked each morning to make giant pans of boiled rice and sausage.
- People in all 78 of Puerto Rico's municipalities ate WCK's food.
- Andrés knew they were not just giving people food. They were giving them hope.

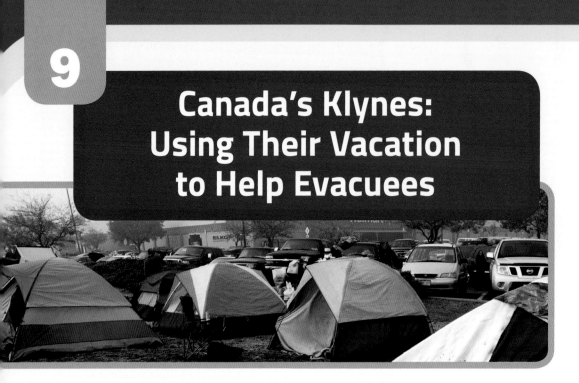

Canada's Klynes: Using Their Vacation to Help Evacuees

Destinee and Paul Klyne wanted a peaceful vacation. They decided to go to Paradise, California. They booked their flight and a place to stay. Then they got bad news. Their vacation cabin had burned down. So had the community around it. Wildfires were spreading throughout northern California.

The Klynes could have stayed home in British Columbia. Instead, they went to California to see how they could help. They found a place to stay in Sacramento. Every day, they drove to Chico, a town outside the fire zone. Many victims had evacuated there. The Klynes asked their friends and family members for donations. They used the money to buy store gift cards. Then they handed them out in the local Walmart parking lot.

10,000
Number of homes destroyed by the Paradise Wildfire

- Hundreds of shops and other buildings burned to the ground.
- Over 600 people were reported missing.
- It was one of the deadliest wildfires in US history.

9

20

Paul Klyne (right) serves food to fire evacuees.

UNBELIEVABLE SIGHTS

The Klynes saw cars with doors that were completely melted. The store parking lot became a city of tents. Most people walked around in a daze. Despite the tragedy, the couple also saw people meeting and hugging. They were showing how happy they were to see their friends alive.

A food truck set up in the same parking lot. The Klynes helped the owner serve meals to evacuees. Before long, the truck ran out of meals. The next day, someone donated $2,000 to stock the truck. More donations poured in. The money bought groceries and filled gas tanks. One day, the Klynes helped feed over 1,000 people. They spent over 11 hours cooking on a grill. They had booked a vacation to pamper themselves. Instead, they spent their time taking care of others.

One America: Raising Millions for Hurricane Victims

OneAmericaAppeal.org
SUPPORT HURRICANE RECOVERY EFFORTS

From left to right: George H. W. Bush, Barack Obama, George W. Bush, Bill Clinton, and Jimmy Carter.

Hurricane Harvey battered Texas in August 2017. More than 1 million people had to flee their homes. The storm caused over $180 billion in damage. Five former presidents joined together to help. They organized the One America Appeal.

On September 7, George H.W. Bush announced the project in a press release. That night, a commercial titled "Our Friends in Texas" aired during the NFL opening game. Bill Clinton, Jimmy Carter, and Barack Obama appeared. So did George H.W. Bush and his son, George W. Bush. They asked for money to help Texans recover from the storm. The presidents set up a website to receive donations.

As they watched Hurricanes Irma and Maria approach US shores, the presidents expanded their appeal. In October, the organization hosted a concert. It was called "Deep from the Heart: The One America Appeal." Stars including Lady Gaga and Lyle Lovett performed. The concert raised $31 million.

The presidents set up a special account through the George H.W. Bush Presidential Library Foundation. One hundred percent of the money raised went to help hurricane victims. Funds were distributed in Texas, Florida, Puerto Rico, and the US Virgin Islands. The One America Appeal ended in December 2017.

$42 million
Amount of money raised by the One America Appeal

- More than 110,000 donors gave to the appeal.
- Major gifts came in from corporations and charities. Donors included the Merck company, the NFL Foundation, and the PGA Tour.
- The former presidents recorded a thank-you message to bring the appeal to a close.

Lady Gaga performing at "Deep from the Heart: The One America Appeal."

Wilma Melville: Training Four-Legged Rescuers

When Wilma Melville returned home to California in 1995, she was exhausted. She and her dog, Murphy, had been searching for survivors of the Oklahoma City bombing. Few victims were found alive. Wilma knew America needed more highly-trained canine search teams. The next year, she founded the National Disaster Search Dog Foundation (SDF). Its mission is to find shelter dogs and pair them with first responders.

As the head of SDF, Wilma enlists human volunteers who share her vision. She visits shelters to find the dogs. Those that are chosen are taken to the SDF center in California. Then the training begins. Wilma and her staff teach the dogs how to look through fields of wreckage. The dogs learn how to alert their handlers when they find a scent. Dogs that show promise meet their handlers after six to nine months of training.

Since the nonprofit began, SDF dogs and handlers have saved lives in over 170 disasters. Thirteen teams searched the rubble of the World Trade Center after the 9/11 attacks. SDF teams were called in after Hurricanes Katrina, Harvey, and Irma. They also rescued disaster victims in Japan, Haiti, and Nepal.

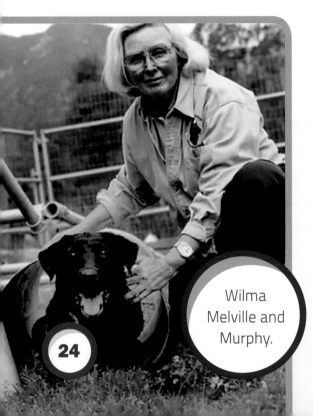

Wilma Melville and Murphy.

Shirley Hammond (above) and dog Sonny Boy were one of the first to reach the World Trade Center after the 9/11 attacks.

168
Number of search teams Wilma planned to train

- In the beginning, her goal was to train one team for each victim of the Oklahoma City bombing. There were 168 victims.
- By early 2019, SDF had trained 210 teams.
- The organization has won several awards for their work.

THEIR NOSES KNOW

A dog's nose makes a good search tool when people are trapped under piles of rubble. But rescue dogs need more than a keen sense of smell. They have to follow commands and be able to deal with distractions. Wilma Melville uses Labrador retrievers, border collies, and German shepherds for SDF search dogs.

Mormon Helping Hands: Teens Work Hard after a Hurricane

MHH volunteers wear the same yellow shirts.

barely knew where to start. But with the help of their adult leaders, they figured it out.

The teens were part of a group called Mormon Helping Hands (MHH). After the storm passed, their church hotline lit up with requests from local residents. The group quickly set up a staging area in a chapel. They began handing out food and water. Then the teens went to work on cleanup.

The teams were armed with saws, tarps, and other supplies. They started cutting up fallen trees and stacking branches. One home needed more than one crew. Three chainsaws were going at the same time. Thirty people worked to stack the wood. Even after

When Hurricane Irma hit Florida in September 2017, teens responded to calls for help. At first, they were overwhelmed. They had never seen such wreckage. Trees were downed. Houses were flooded. The teens

working all day, they couldn't finish the job. They had to return the next day to get it done.

The volunteers cleared out houses flooded by the storm surge. They dragged heavy, muddy furniture and mattresses. Everything was ruined. But the teens noticed something. Though they had lost everything, the people had hope. They were glad to be alive. And they were grateful for the teens' help.

66
Cases of peanut butter distributed by Mormon Helping Hands

- Several truckloads of food and supplies arrived in South Florida.
- Volunteers handed out over 80 cases of baby cereal.
- The trucks also carried equipment needed to help with the cleanup.

THINK ABOUT IT

The MHH teens did what they could to help victims of Irma. When they got tired, they sat down and handed out snacks and water. Would you be willing to take the time to help as they did? What jobs could you do?

Ways You Can Help

- Donate clothes you don't need. Make sure they are clean. Take them to an organization that is collecting them. They will send them where they need to go.

- Donate money. Have an adult help you find an organization you want to support. Then give part of your allowance or savings. Organize a bake sale or sell lemonade and give the money you make.

- Animals are affected by disasters, too. Contact an animal shelter to see if they need donations of pet food or money.

- After a disaster, many people have to stay in shelters or hospitals for a period of time. Maybe they don't have homes to return to. Maybe they're sick or injured. Make cards or write letters of encouragement. Ask an adult to help you decide where to send them.

- If a shelter is close by, ask an adult to take you there. Bring books and games. Read and play with younger children.

- Collect cleaning supplies and donate them to a local shelter. People will need them when they return to their homes.

- Start a local food drive. Sort and box all the donations you receive. Give them to an organization that is helping.

Glossary

debris
Pieces that are left when something is destroyed.

devastated
Greatly harmed or damaged.

distractions
Things that make it hard to think or pay attention.

foundation
An organization that uses donated money to help society.

hygiene
Things a person does to stay clean and healthy.

political
Relating to the government.

polymer
A natural or human-made substance with molecules that are linked together.

press release
An official statement given to members of the news media.

reinvented
Made changes or improvements to something.

trauma
A serious injury to a person's body.

waive
To give up something you have a legal right to, like a fee for a service.

Read More

Peters, Stephanie. *Superpower Dogs: Halo: Disaster Response Dog*. New York: Little Brown and Company, 2019.

Holmes, Kirsty. *Médecins Sans Frontières: Doctors Without Borders*. World Charities. King's Lynn, England: BookLife, 2018.

Marsico, Katie. *UNICEF*. How Do They Help? Ann Arbor, MI: Cherry Lake Publishing, 2015.

Visit 12StoryLibrary.com

Scan the code or use your school's login at **12StoryLibrary.com** for recent updates about this topic and a full digital version of this book. Enjoy free access to:

- Digital ebook
- Breaking news updates
- Live content feeds
- Videos, interactive maps, and graphics
- Additional web resources

Note to educators: Visit 12StoryLibrary.com/register to sign up for free premium website access. Enjoy live content plus a full digital version of every 12-Story Library book you own for every student at your school.

Index

About the Author

Patricia Hutchison is a former teacher. She has written dozens of nonfiction children's books about science, nature, history, and geography. She lives in South Carolina with her husband. They love to travel throughout the United States and to other countries.